The Pirates!
In an Adventure
with SCIENTISTS!

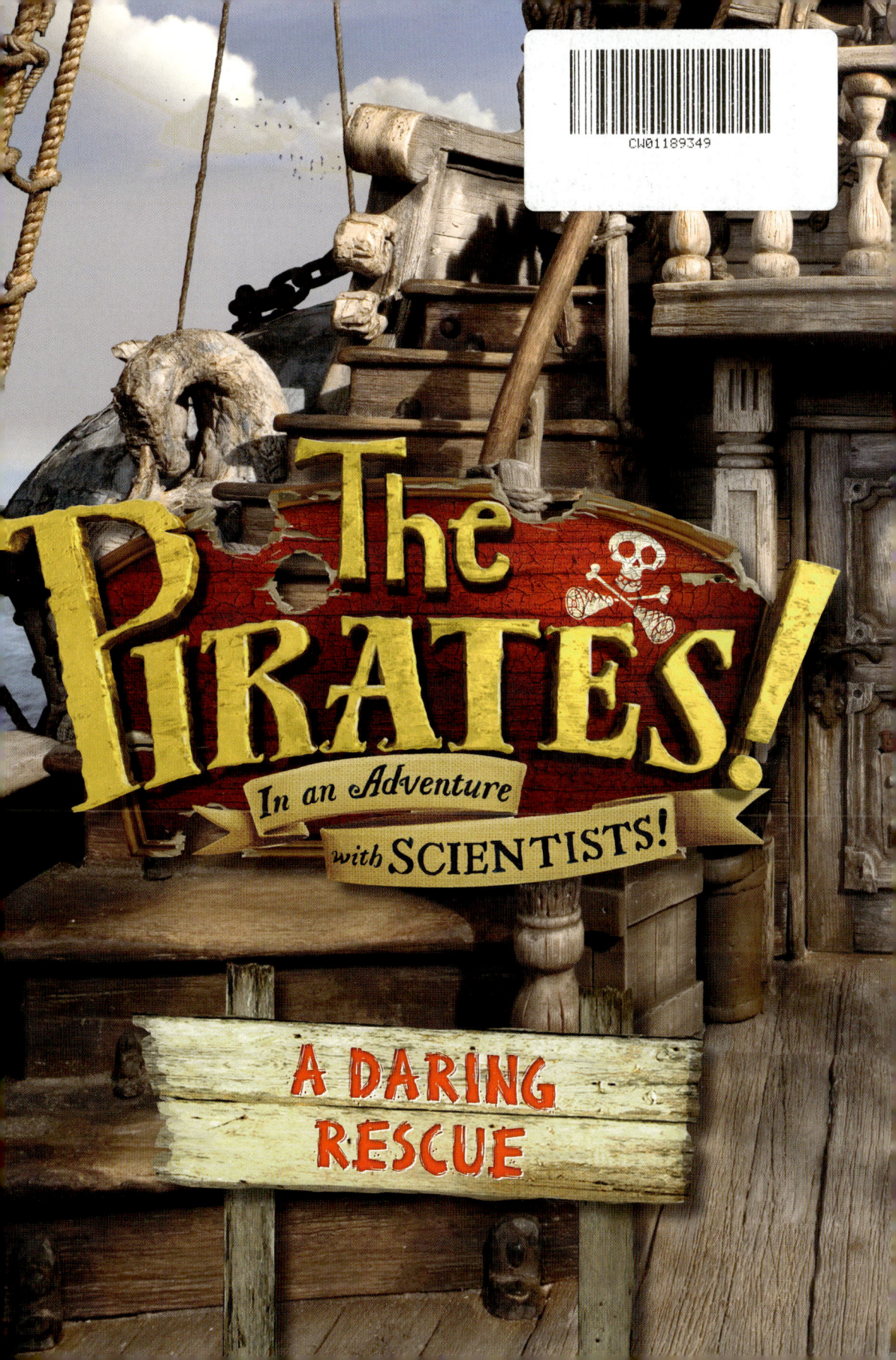

A DARING RESCUE

Published by Pearson Education Limited, Edinburgh Gate, Harlow, Essex, CM20 2JE.

www.pearsonschools.co.uk

™ & © 2013 Sony Pictures Animation Inc. All rights reserved.
Excerpted and adapted from the novel and screenplay by Gideon Defoe.

Layout by Andy Magee
New text by Helen Parker

First published 2013

17 16 15
10 9 8 7 6 5 4 3 2

British Library Cataloguing in Publication Data
A catalogue record for this book is available from the British Library

ISBN 978 0 435 14388 6

Copyright notice

All rights reserved. No part of this publication may be reproduced in any form or by any means (including photocopying or storing it in any medium by electronic means and whether or not transiently or incidentally to some other use of this publication) without the written permission of the copyright owner, except in accordance with the provisions of the Copyright, Designs and Patents Act 1988 or under the terms of a licence issued by the Copyright Licensing Agency, Saffron House, 6–10 Kirby Street, London EC1N 8TS (www.cla.co.uk). Applications for the copyright owner's written permission should be addressed to the publisher.

Printed and bound in China (CTPS)

Acknowledgements

We would like to thank Bangor Central Integrated Primary School, Northern Ireland; Bishop Henderson Church of England Primary School, Somerset; Bletchingdon Parochial Church of England Primary School, Oxfordshire; Brookside Community Primary School, Somerset; Bude Park Primary School, Hull; Carisbrooke Church of England Primary School, Isle of Wight; Cheddington Combined School, Buckinghamshire; Dair House Independent School, Buckinghamshire; Glebe Infant School, Gloucestershire; Henley Green Primary School, Coventry; Lovelace Primary School, Surrey; Our Lady of Peace Junior School, Slough; Tackley Church of England Primary School, Oxfordshire; and Twyford Church of England School, Buckinghamshire for their invaluable help in the development and trialling of the Bug Club resources.

Every effort has been made to contact copyright holders of material reproduced in this book. Any omissions will be rectified in subsequent printings if notice is given to the publishers.

Contents

Chapter 1
The Pirate of the Year Awards 4

Chapter 2
A Nasty Surprise 7

Chapter 3
The Pirate Captain Goes to London ... 12

Chapter 4
Off to Save Polly 17

Chapter 5
Dinner is Served 21

Chapter 6
A Fierce Battle 28

Chapter 7
A Very Fizzy Mess 33

Chapter 8
A Daring Rescue 36

Chapter 1
The Pirate of the Year Awards

On Blood Island, pirates from all over the world were gathering for the annual Pirate of the Year Awards.

The Pirate Captain was at the show with his trusty crew, and this year he knew he would win. He had always dreamed of winning, but he had always failed. This year was different though. This year, the Pirate Captain knew he had *much* more treasure than any other pirate in the competition!

As the Pirate Captain and his crew sat down at their table, one of the crew asked, "Please can Polly come out now?"

"Best not; she's still tired from the trip," replied the Pirate Captain.

He was lying. Not long ago, a scientist had told the Pirate Captain that Polly was not a parrot, but a rare and valuable dodo. The Pirate Captain had then secretly sold Polly to the Queen of England in exchange for masses of treasure.

Just then the Pirate King, who was presenting the show, jumped onto the stage. The crowd fell silent.

"The judges have counted each pirate's treasure …" the Pirate King announced, "and this year's winner is … the Pirate Captain!"

The Pirate Captain leaped onto the stage with his arms raised in the air as the crowd of pirates clapped and cheered. He'd finally done it! He'd won!

Chapter 2
A Nasty Surprise

The Pirate Captain was reaching out to collect his trophy from the Pirate King when suddenly another pirate, Black Bellamy, stood up. He held out a newspaper with a picture of the Pirate Captain on the front.

"The Queen of England has *pardoned* the Pirate Captain," Black Bellamy shouted. "That means that the Queen of England has forgiven him ... and if he has been forgiven by the Queen, who *hates* all pirates, he is no longer one of us! If you are not a pirate, you can't win the award!"

The Pirate Captain's dream had turned into a nightmare. Not only had he lost the competition, but it seemed that he could no longer be a pirate either.

"Hand over your pirate clothes and all of your treasure," said the Pirate King.

Reluctantly, the Pirate Captain handed everything over.

"Now leave Blood Island for ever!" bellowed the Pirate King. "You are a pirate no more."

With that, the Pirate Captain and his crew were thrown out onto the street.

"Don't worry," said one of crew. "We don't need them and their silly awards."

"Yes," said another. "Everyone knows the best thing about being a pirate isn't the treasure. It's the swords, and party night, and Polly!"

The crew nodded and cheered in agreement. But where *was* Polly? They hadn't seen her for ages. And *why* had the Pirate Captain been pardoned?

"Where *is* Polly, Captain?" asked one of the smaller pirates.

"I've told you," said the Pirate Captain. "She's hiding in my beard."

It was clear the crew didn't believe him. He sighed; he could lie to them no more.

"Okay, okay. I sold Polly to the Queen of England in return for a boatload of treasure," the Pirate Captain admitted.

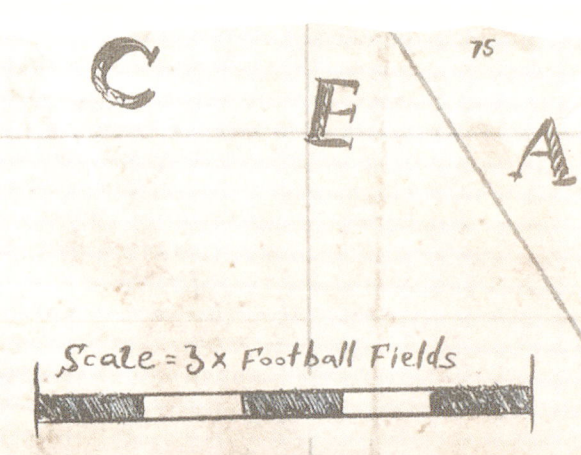

The crew stared at him in disbelief.

"But ... she was *our* Polly!" said one crew member. "She was a member of the family – the life and soul of the ship!"

One by one, they turned their backs on the Pirate Captain and walked away.

The Pirate Captain turned to Number Two. "Ha! Looks like it's you and me now, Number Two." But Number Two shook his head, turned his back and walked away too.

Chapter 3
The Pirate Captain Goes to London

The crew had abandoned the Pirate Captain. He had lost everything, and he felt terrible about letting everyone down. He had been so focused on the prize that he had betrayed his crew.

Right then and there, he decided that he must return to London and get Polly back!

When the Pirate Captain arrived in London, he headed for the Royal Petting Zoo. The gate of the zoo was locked, so the Pirate Captain jumped over the wall.

Disguising himself as a tree, he crept across the zoo to the cage where Polly was kept, but when he arrived, it was empty.

"You're too late. She's gone," a voice called from behind him. It was the Scientist, with his pet monkey, Mr Bobo.

"What are you doing here?" asked the Pirate Captain. "And where's Polly?"

"Oh, it's too horrible," the Scientist replied, and handed over a menu. On the front of the menu it read: 'Banquet for World Leaders'.

The Pirate Captain started reading the menu and was shocked to see that the main course was 'dodo'.

"I don't understand. What is this?" asked the Pirate Captain.

"I found out that the Queen is a member of a terrible, secret dining club," the Scientist explained. "Every year, kings and queens from around the world meet in her ship to eat the most endangered creatures they can find. And this year the main course is … Polly!"

The Pirate Captain gasped. "You mean she's going to *eat* Polly?"

The Scientist nodded.

"Well, we've got to rescue her!" said the Pirate Captain.

"Surely it's impossible!" said the Scientist, but he agreed to try anyway. At that moment, Mr Bobo ran off.

"This mission isn't for everyone," said the Scientist sadly, as he watched Mr Bobo running away.

Chapter 4
Off to Save Polly

The Pirate Captain and the Scientist needed to find the Queen's ship as soon as possible, but the Captain no longer had a boat. His crew had taken it when they left him.

Luckily, the Scientist had a friend who owned an airship, so they borrowed it and were soon flying over London. The Scientist pedalled, while the Pirate Captain gave directions.

They flew the airship thousands of miles over land and sea, and through all different types of weather.

As the Scientist pedalled and pedalled, the Pirate Captain warmed his hands by the stove and looked through his telescope for the Queen's ship.

Finally, as they flew across the Pacific Ocean, an enormous ship loomed up behind them, almost knocking them out of the air.

"That's it!" cried the Pirate Captain.
"But how can we get on board?" asked the Scientist.

The Pirate Captain had a cunning plan. He tied a rope to the Scientist and threw him overboard onto the ship. The rope pulled down the airship, which landed with a CRASH on the deck.

"Fantastic!" cried the Pirate Captain. "Now, let's find Polly!"

Chapter 5
Dinner is Served

Inside the ship's dining room, the Queen was sitting with her guests. They were finishing the first course of their dinner.

"How was the first course, Your Majesty?" asked one of the guests.

"Mmmm, quite tasty," said the Queen, "but just wait until you see what we've got for the main course!"

The Queen called to her chef through her speaking tube, "We're ready for the main course now!"

She was overheard by the Pirate Captain and the Scientist, who were spying through a porthole into the dining room.

"She's called for the main course – there's not a moment to lose!" cried the Pirate Captain. "We must find the kitchen!"

Meanwhile, in the ship's kitchen, the chef was busy unlocking a storeroom where all of the rare creatures were imprisoned.

He opened Polly's cage and lifted her out but, as he was walking over to the oven, the Pirate Captain hit him with a rolling pin.

The chef fell down and dropped Polly.

The Pirate Captain saw his chance and, picking up Polly, he hugged her tightly.

"I'm sorry, old girl," he said. "I will never leave you again, I promise!"

Just then they heard the Queen's voice on the speaking tube, calling for the chef.

"Chef! Hello? Where is my dodo?" the Queen cried down the speaking tube.

The Pirate Captain couldn't resist a bit of fun, so he replied pretending to be the chef. "You cannot hurry the cooking of the dodo, Your Majesty," he said. "It is a very delicate recipe."

The Pirate Captain was so busy pretending to be the chef that he didn't notice the Queen creeping up on them.

"Um … Captain …" said the Scientist.

The Captain spun around and came face to face with the Queen.

"The Pirate Captain and the Scientist. Here you are again!" she said.

The Queen pushed the Scientist out of the way and walked towards the Pirate Captain.

"Give me my dodo!" she screamed, brandishing a frying pan.

"Maybe we can talk about this ..." said the Pirate Captain, as he grabbed another big frying pan.

The Queen didn't want to talk; she wanted to fight!

Chapter 6
A Fierce Battle

Suddenly, the Queen threw away her frying pan and two metal doors opened in her skirt. She pulled out two long swords and began twirling them as she ran towards the Captain, performing a series of jumps and spins.

The Captain managed to knock the swords out of her hands, but he was no match for the furious Queen!

She jumped up into the air, swung from a rack and knocked Polly out of the Captain's grasp.

"You're going to taste delicious," cried the Queen as she caught Polly.

She was just about to put Polly into the oven when out of nowhere Mr Bobo, the Scientist's pet monkey, swung across the kitchen on a rope.

He grabbed Polly out of the Queen's hands and landed safely on the other side of the room.

"Give me back my dinner!" the Queen screeched.

At that moment, Number Two burst in and threw a sword to the Pirate Captain. The Captain caught the sword and cut a rope that was holding up some vinegar barrels just above the Queen's head.

The barrels tumbled down towards the Queen, knocking her backwards into a storeroom full of baking powder.

"Good work, Number Two!" cried the Pirate Captain. "Are the rest of the crew on board? How did you find me?"

"They're all on board," Number Two replied. "Mr Bobo told us where you were. He rowed halfway across the ocean to tell us what you were up to and we thought you might need a bit of help. After all, we are your crew and we did have the ship!"

The Pirate Captain looked ashamed. "Listen, Number Two," he said. "I let you down badly and I'm very sorry. And now it seems I'm doing something even more stupid on board this ship …"

"But you're rescuing Polly now!" said Number Two. "And that's the reason why the crew and I still think you're the best pirate to sail the seven seas!"

Chapter 7
A Very Fizzy Mess

The crew were celebrating getting Polly back when they heard a strange fizzing noise.

They turned to see where the noise was coming from. The doors of the baking powder storeroom suddenly flew open and the Queen shot out, carried on a giant wave of white foam. (As every good scientist knows, baking powder mixed with vinegar creates a very bubbly explosion!)

As the wave of foam surged past the Captain, the Queen snatched Polly out of his hands. The wave then carried the Captain and his crew out of the kitchen and up onto the deck.

Soon the whole ship was full of foam!

The Queen fled from the foam with Polly under her arm. The Pirate Captain gave chase. When the Queen saw the airship that the Pirate Captain and the Scientist had used, she raced towards it.

"Oh no you don't …" cried the Pirate Captain. But it was too late. The Queen untied the airship and jumped on board.

Chapter 8
A Daring Rescue

"Say goodbye to your dodo!" cried the Queen, as she flew up into the sky.

At that moment, the Pirate Captain saw a rope trailing from the airship. Bravely, he leaped into the air and grabbed the rope.

As the airship rose into the sky, the Pirate Captain dangled below it.

The Queen was furious and tried to get Polly to cut the rope.

"Bite it, you stupid bird!" she shrieked, but Polly refused as she was loyal to the Pirate Captain. Instead, she bit the Queen on the nose!

As the Queen staggered back in shock, her crown punctured the airship, which began to spin wildly. Polly tried to keep her balance, but soon tumbled from the side.

Luckily, she was caught by the Pirate Captain, who was still dangling below! The crew then helped the Pirate Captain and Polly from the swinging rope back onto their own ship.

"You'll pay for this!" the Queen shouted down from the airship.

"Does that mean he is no longer pardoned?" Number Two called out.

"Of course he's no longer pardoned!" the Queen screamed, as the airship zipped away.

Back on board the pirate ship, everyone cheered. The Captain was a pirate again, and the true winner of the Pirate of the Year Award.

The Pirate Captain was delighted to be back on board his ship where he belonged.

"Welcome back, Captain!" Number Two cried, and everyone cheered once more.

"Let's set a course for adventure!" boomed the Captain.

"Aye, aye, Captain!" the crew shouted excitedly, and sailed off into the sunset.